FINDING HOPE
& HEALING
IN THE MIDST
OF GRIEF

A JOURNAL FOR THE
BROKEN HEARTED

FINDING HOPE & HEALING

_____

_____

_____

_____

_____

_____

_____

_____

_____

_____

_____

_____

_____

_____

_____

_____

_____

_____

Equipping Souls for Life After Loss

FINDING HOPE & HEALING

Equipping Souls for Life After Loss

FINDING HOPE & HEALING

_____

_____

_____

_____

_____

_____

_____

_____

_____

_____

_____

_____

_____

_____

_____

_____

_____

Equipping Souls for Life After Loss

FINDING HOPE & HEALING

_____

_____

_____

_____

_____

_____

_____

_____

_____

_____

_____

_____

_____

_____

_____

_____

_____

_____

_____

_____

Equipping Souls for Life After Loss

FINDING HOPE & HEALING

Equipping Souls for Life After Loss

FINDING HOPE & HEALING

_____

_____

_____

_____

_____

_____

_____

_____

_____

_____

_____

_____

_____

_____

_____

_____

_____

_____

_____

Equipping Souls for Life After Loss

FINDING HOPE & HEALING

Equipping Souls for Life After Loss

FINDING HOPE & HEALING

_____

_____

_____

_____

_____

_____

_____

_____

_____

_____

_____

_____

_____

_____

_____

_____

Equipping Souls for Life After Loss

FINDING HOPE & HEALING

_____

_____

_____

_____

_____

_____

_____

_____

_____

_____

_____

_____

_____

_____

_____

_____

_____

_____

Equipping Souls for Life After Loss

FINDING HOPE & HEALING

_____

_____

_____

_____

_____

_____

_____

_____

_____

_____

_____

_____

_____

_____

_____

_____

Equipping Souls for Life After Loss

FINDING HOPE & HEALING

_____

_____

_____

_____

_____

_____

_____

_____

_____

_____

_____

_____

_____

_____

_____

_____

_____

_____

Equipping Souls for Life After Loss

FINDING HOPE & HEALING

_____

_____

_____

_____

_____

_____

_____

_____

_____

_____

_____

_____

_____

_____

_____

_____

_____

Equipping Souls for Life After Loss

FINDING HOPE & HEALING

_____

_____

_____

_____

_____

_____

_____

_____

_____

_____

_____

_____

_____

_____

_____

_____

_____

Equipping Souls for Life After Loss

FINDING HOPE & HEALING

_____

_____

_____

_____

_____

_____

_____

_____

_____

_____

_____

_____

_____

_____

_____

_____

_____

_____

Equipping Souls for Life After Loss

FINDING HOPE & HEALING

_____

_____

_____

_____

_____

_____

_____

_____

_____

_____

_____

_____

_____

_____

_____

_____

_____

Equipping Souls for Life After Loss

FINDING HOPE & HEALING

_____

_____

_____

_____

_____

_____

_____

_____

_____

_____

_____

_____

_____

_____

_____

_____

_____

_____

_____

FINDING HOPE & HEALING

_____

_____

_____

_____

_____

_____

_____

_____

_____

_____

_____

_____

_____

_____

_____

_____

_____

_____

FINDING HOPE & HEALING

_____

_____

_____

_____

_____

_____

_____

_____

_____

_____

_____

_____

_____

_____

_____

_____

_____

Equipping Souls for Life After Loss

FINDING HOPE & HEALING

_____

_____

_____

_____

_____

_____

_____

_____

_____

_____

_____

_____

_____

_____

_____

_____

_____

_____

Equipping Souls for Life After Loss

FINDING HOPE & HEALING

Equipping Souls for Life After Loss

FINDING HOPE & HEALING

_____

_____

_____

_____

_____

_____

_____

_____

_____

_____

_____

_____

_____

_____

_____

_____

_____

_____

_____

_____

_____

Equipping Souls for Life After Loss

FINDING HOPE & HEALING

Equipping Souls for Life After Loss

FINDING HOPE & HEALING

Equipping Souls for Life After Loss

FINDING HOPE & HEALING

_____

_____

_____

_____

_____

_____

_____

_____

_____

_____

_____

_____

_____

_____

_____

_____

Equipping Souls for Life After Loss

FINDING HOPE & HEALING

Equipping Souls for Life After Loss

FINDING HOPE & HEALING

Equipping Souls for Life After Loss

FINDING HOPE & HEALING

_____

_____

_____

_____

_____

_____

_____

_____

_____

_____

_____

_____

_____

_____

_____

_____

_____

_____

_____

Equipping Souls for Life After Loss

FINDING HOPE & HEALING

_____
_____
_____
_____
_____
_____
_____
_____
_____
_____
_____
_____
_____
_____
_____
_____
_____
_____

Equipping Souls for Life After Loss

FINDING HOPE & HEALING

_____

_____

_____

_____

_____

_____

_____

_____

_____

_____

_____

_____

_____

_____

_____

_____

_____

_____

_____

_____

Equipping Souls for Life After Loss

FINDING HOPE & HEALING

_____

_____

_____

_____

_____

_____

_____

_____

_____

_____

_____

_____

_____

_____

_____

Equipping Souls for Life After Loss

FINDING HOPE & HEALING

Equipping Souls for Life After Loss

FINDING HOPE & HEALING

_____

_____

_____

_____

_____

_____

_____

_____

_____

_____

_____

_____

_____

_____

_____

_____

_____

Equipping Souls for Life After Loss

FINDING HOPE & HEALING

_____

_____

_____

_____

_____

_____

_____

_____

_____

_____

_____

_____

_____

_____

_____

_____

_____

_____

Equipping Souls for Life After Loss

FINDING HOPE & HEALING

Equipping Souls for Life After Loss

FINDING HOPE & HEALING

_____

_____

_____

_____

_____

_____

_____

_____

_____

_____

_____

_____

_____

_____

_____

_____

_____

_____

_____

Equipping Souls for Life After Loss

FINDING HOPE & HEALING

_____

_____

_____

_____

_____

_____

_____

_____

_____

_____

_____

_____

_____

_____

_____

Equipping Souls for Life After Loss

FINDING HOPE & HEALING

Equipping Souls for Life After Loss

FINDING HOPE & HEALING

_____

_____

_____

_____

_____

_____

_____

_____

_____

_____

_____

_____

_____

_____

_____

_____

_____

_____

Equipping Souls for Life After Loss

FINDING HOPE & HEALING

Equipping Souls for Life After Loss

FINDING HOPE & HEALING

_____
_____
_____
_____
_____
_____
_____
_____
_____
_____
_____
_____
_____
_____
_____
_____
_____
_____

Equipping Souls for Life After Loss

FINDING HOPE & HEALING

_____
_____
_____
_____
_____
_____
_____
_____
_____
_____
_____
_____
_____
_____
_____
_____
_____
_____
_____
_____

Equipping Souls for Life After Loss

FINDING HOPE & HEALING

Equipping Souls for Life After Loss

FINDING HOPE & HEALING

_____

_____

_____

_____

_____

_____

_____

_____

_____

_____

_____

_____

_____

_____

_____

_____

Equipping Souls for Life After Loss

FINDING HOPE & HEALING

_____

_____

_____

_____

_____

_____

_____

_____

_____

_____

_____

_____

_____

_____

_____

_____

_____

Equipping Souls for Life After Loss

FINDING HOPE & HEALING

_____

_____

_____

_____

_____

_____

_____

_____

_____

_____

_____

_____

_____

_____

_____

_____

_____

_____

_____

Equipping Souls for Life After Loss

FINDING HOPE & HEALING

Equipping Souls for Life After Loss

FINDING HOPE & HEALING

Equipping Souls for Life After Loss

FINDING HOPE & HEALING

_____

_____

_____

_____

_____

_____

_____

_____

_____

_____

_____

_____

_____

_____

_____

_____

Equipping Souls for Life After Loss

FINDING HOPE & HEALING

Equipping Souls for Life After Loss

FINDING HOPE & HEALING

_____

_____

_____

_____

_____

_____

_____

_____

_____

_____

_____

_____

_____

_____

_____

_____

_____

_____

FINDING HOPE & HEALING

_____

_____

_____

_____

_____

_____

_____

_____

_____

_____

_____

_____

_____

_____

_____

_____

_____

_____

_____

_____

_____

Equipping Souls for Life After Loss

FINDING HOPE & HEALING

FINDING HOPE & HEALING

_____

_____

_____

_____

_____

_____

_____

_____

_____

_____

_____

_____

_____

_____

_____

_____

_____

_____

Equipping Souls for Life After Loss

FINDING HOPE & HEALING

_____

_____

_____

_____

_____

_____

_____

_____

_____

_____

_____

_____

_____

_____

_____

_____

_____

Equipping Souls for Life After Loss

FINDING HOPE & HEALING

FINDING HOPE & HEALING

_____

_____

_____

_____

_____

_____

_____

_____

_____

_____

_____

_____

_____

_____

_____

_____

_____

Equipping Souls for Life After Loss

FINDING HOPE & HEALING

_____

_____

_____

_____

_____

_____

_____

_____

_____

_____

_____

_____

_____

_____

_____

_____

_____

_____

_____

_____

Equipping Souls for Life After Loss

FINDING HOPE & HEALING

_____

_____

_____

_____

_____

_____

_____

_____

_____

_____

_____

_____

_____

_____

_____

_____

_____

Equipping Souls for Life After Loss

FINDING HOPE & HEALING

Equipping Souls for Life After Loss

FINDING HOPE & HEALING

_____

_____

_____

_____

_____

_____

_____

_____

_____

_____

_____

_____

_____

_____

_____

_____

_____

_____

Equipping Souls for Life After Loss

FINDING HOPE & HEALING

Equipping Souls for Life After Loss

FINDING HOPE & HEALING

_____

_____

_____

_____

_____

_____

_____

_____

_____

_____

_____

_____

_____

_____

_____

_____

Equipping Souls for Life After Loss

FINDING HOPE & HEALING

_____

_____

_____

_____

_____

_____

_____

_____

_____

_____

_____

_____

_____

_____

_____

_____

_____

_____

_____

Equipping Souls for Life After Loss

FINDING HOPE & HEALING

Equipping Souls for Life After Loss

FINDING HOPE & HEALING

_____

_____

_____

_____

_____

_____

_____

_____

_____

_____

_____

_____

_____

_____

_____

_____

_____

_____

_____

Equipping Souls for Life After Loss

FINDING HOPE & HEALING

_____

_____

_____

_____

_____

_____

_____

_____

_____

_____

_____

_____

_____

_____

_____

_____

_____

_____

Equipping Souls for Life After Loss

FINDING HOPE & HEALING

Equipping Souls for Life After Loss

FINDING HOPE & HEALING

Equipping Souls for Life After Loss

FINDING HOPE & HEALING

Equipping Souls for Life After Loss

FINDING HOPE & HEALING

Equipping Souls for Life After Loss

FINDING HOPE & HEALING

_____

_____

_____

_____

_____

_____

_____

_____

_____

_____

_____

_____

_____

_____

_____

_____

_____

_____

Equipping Souls for Life After Loss

FINDING HOPE & HEALING

_____

_____

_____

_____

_____

_____

_____

_____

_____

_____

_____

_____

_____

_____

_____

_____

Equipping Souls for Life After Loss

FINDING HOPE & HEALING

_____

_____

_____

_____

_____

_____

_____

_____

_____

_____

_____

_____

_____

_____

_____

_____

_____

_____

_____

_____

Equipping Souls for Life After Loss

FINDING HOPE & HEALING

_____

_____

_____

_____

_____

_____

_____

_____

_____

_____

_____

_____

_____

_____

_____

_____

_____

_____

_____

Equipping Souls for Life After Loss

FINDING HOPE & HEALING

Equipping Souls for Life After Loss

FINDING HOPE & HEALING

Equipping Souls for Life After Loss

FINDING HOPE & HEALING

_____

_____

_____

_____

_____

_____

_____

_____

_____

_____

_____

_____

_____

_____

_____

_____

_____

_____

_____

Equipping Souls for Life After Loss

FINDING HOPE & HEALING

Equipping Souls for Life After Loss

FINDING HOPE & HEALING

_____

_____

_____

_____

_____

_____

_____

_____

_____

_____

_____

_____

_____

_____

_____

_____

_____

_____

_____

Equipping Souls for Life After Loss

FINDING HOPE & HEALING

Equipping Souls for Life After Loss

FINDING HOPE & HEALING

Equipping Souls for Life After Loss

FINDING HOPE & HEALING

_____

_____

_____

_____

_____

_____

_____

_____

_____

_____

_____

_____

_____

_____

_____

_____

_____

Equipping Souls for Life After Loss

FINDING HOPE & HEALING

Equipping Souls for Life After Loss

FINDING HOPE & HEALING

Equipping Souls for Life After Loss

FINDING HOPE & HEALING

Equipping Souls for Life After Loss

FINDING HOPE & HEALING

_____
_____
_____
_____
_____
_____
_____
_____
_____
_____
_____
_____
_____
_____
_____
_____
_____

Equipping Souls for Life After Loss

FINDING HOPE & HEALING

_____

_____

_____

_____

_____

_____

_____

_____

_____

_____

_____

_____

_____

_____

_____

_____

_____

_____

Equipping Souls for Life After Loss

FINDING HOPE & HEALING

_____

_____

_____

_____

_____

_____

_____

_____

_____

_____

_____

_____

_____

_____

_____

_____

_____

_____

Equipping Souls for Life After Loss

FINDING HOPE & HEALING

Equipping Souls for Life After Loss

FINDING HOPE & HEALING

_____

_____

_____

_____

_____

_____

_____

_____

_____

_____

_____

_____

_____

_____

_____

_____

_____

Equipping Souls for Life After Loss

FINDING HOPE & HEALING

_____

_____

_____

_____

_____

_____

_____

_____

_____

_____

_____

_____

_____

_____

_____

_____

_____

Equipping Souls for Life After Loss

FINDING HOPE & HEALING

_____

_____

_____

_____

_____

_____

_____

_____

_____

_____

_____

_____

_____

_____

_____

_____

_____

Equipping Souls for Life After Loss

FINDING HOPE & HEALING

_____

_____

_____

_____

_____

_____

_____

_____

_____

_____

_____

_____

_____

_____

_____

_____

_____

_____

_____

_____

Equipping Souls for Life After Loss

FINDING HOPE & HEALING

_____

_____

_____

_____

_____

_____

_____

_____

_____

_____

_____

_____

_____

_____

_____

_____

_____

_____

Equipping Souls for Life After Loss

FINDING HOPE & HEALING

_____

_____

_____

_____

_____

_____

_____

_____

_____

_____

_____

_____

_____

_____

_____

_____

Equipping Souls for Life After Loss

FINDING HOPE & HEALING

_____

_____

_____

_____

_____

_____

_____

_____

_____

_____

_____

_____

_____

_____

_____

_____

Equipping Souls for Life After Loss

FINDING HOPE & HEALING

_____

_____

_____

_____

_____

_____

_____

_____

_____

_____

_____

_____

_____

_____

_____

_____

_____

_____

_____

Equipping Souls for Life After Loss

FINDING HOPE & HEALING

_____

_____

_____

_____

_____

_____

_____

_____

_____

_____

_____

_____

_____

_____

_____

_____

_____

_____

Equipping Souls for Life After Loss

FINDING HOPE & HEALING

Equipping Souls for Life After Loss

FINDING HOPE & HEALING

Equipping Souls for Life After Loss

THE GRIEF MENTOR

with Teresa Davis

A PODCAST

for the grieving heart

www.thegriefmentor.com

https://www.facebook.com/griefmentor/

www.instagram.com/griefmentor

Made in the USA
Middletown, DE
28 March 2022

63263058R00057